Minecraft: Secrets Handbook

Table of Contents

Introduction

Minecraft has been around for 7 years now and is considered to be among the most beloved games on the Internet.

Simple in design and structure, Minecraft has developed vastly over time with five different game modes.

Luckily different gaming platforms have made the game available on smartphones and the Xbox 360 as well.

With so many options, it's easy to take your pick and play the game in any mode or platform which suits you best.

Minecraft launched an Android version on October 7th, 2011 shortly followed with an iOS version on November 17th, 2011.

Known as Minecraft Pocket edition, the game offers you the same gaming modes as the PC version of the game.

Among the game modes, you get, you can choose from:

- Creative,

- Survival,

- Adventure,

- Spectator,

- Hardcore.

While Minecraft is pretty simple, the Pocket edition is challenging, particularly since you don't have the mouse and keyboard available for commands.

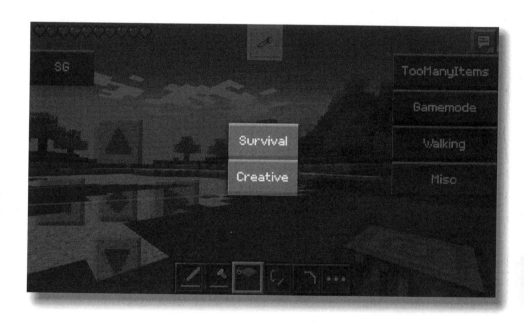

Now whether you're a veteran player or you are just starting out, Minecraft has plenty of hidden secrets in the game.

From crafting to building, there are loads of tricks you can apply to make your game play fun, unique and exciting.

Infinite Water

If you're having a hard time finding water or your water sources is too far away from your home, you can build an infinite source of water near your home.

All you have to do is to dig a hole (2x2) and put water in it. Place them in opposite corners. Now you can use as much water as you need without running out.

Upside Down or Right Side Up?

Creative mode allows you to spawn any kind of mob you want. If you are feeling extra creative, use an Anvil and rename any spawn egg in your inventory.

Naming a spawn egg 'Grumm' will cause any mob to appear upside down!

The Redstone Connection

Using redstone is tricky but there are some neat ways you can hide your redstone trail.

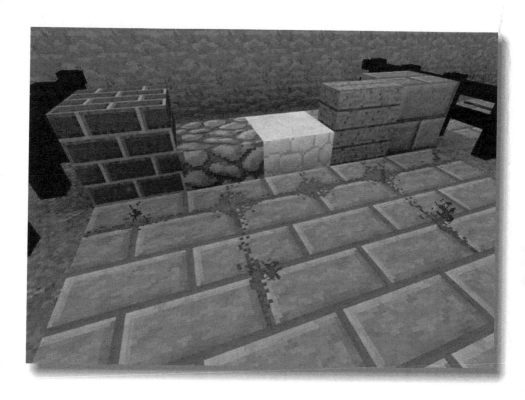

Half slabs can be used to hide redstone as the current is not disrupted because of it. On the other hand, full blocks will still break the current.

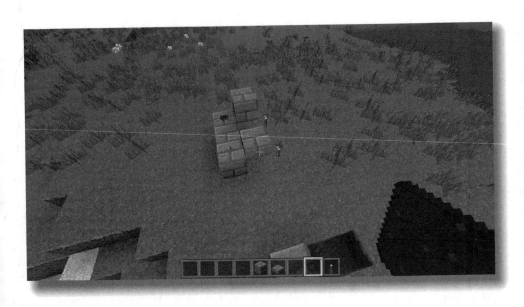

Redstone Lamps

Activated redstone lamps can also activate other lamps if they are touching each other.

You will also need to connect them with a torch or other light source for them to be functional.

Automatic Redstone Lamps

Using redstone lamps, you can create an automatic night light since there is a daylight sensor added to Minecraft.

It may get a little tricky if you're new at working with redstone but once you get the hang of it, this shouldn't be difficult for you.

Mob Revolt

Minecraft monsters may be gruesome but they do look out for each other.

If you injure a Zombie Pigman and there are others around it, they will gang up on you to attack.

Don't Mess with the Wolf Pack

Similarly, if you're trying to tame a wolf but you accidentally hit, you better run away as quickly as you can.

Not only will angry wolves be untameable, if there are other wolves around, the whole pack will band together to hurt you.

Magic Plates

Pressure plates have tons of uses in the Minecraft universe.

Don't Step Too Close Now

Not only are they great for making bobby traps, you can also activate a pressure plate from far away by using a bow and arrow.

Pressure Locks

If you are particularly good with redstone, pressure plates can be used to make automated doors, traps and even a mine cart track.

Pressure Some Lava or Water

You can also use pressure plates to contain water or lava. Plates placed all around the one block of water or lava will stay in place.

If you want to try this trick, just remember to put the plates down first and add the water or lava in the end.

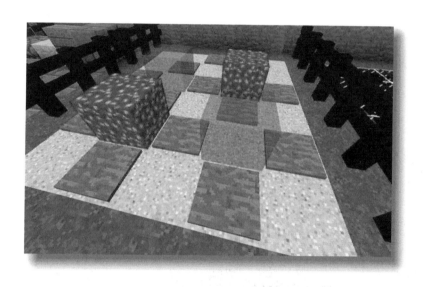

Extreme Fuel

If you're looking for a good source of fuel, you can't

go wrong some of these tricks.

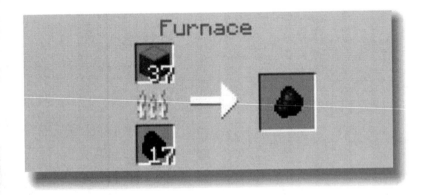

Got a Bucket Full of Lava

One bucket of lava can fuel a furnace for 1000 seconds and allow you to smelt or cook around 1000 items.

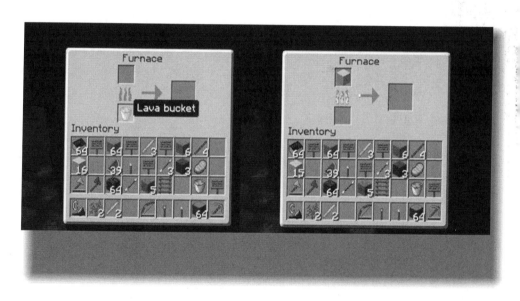

Fire up Some Blaze Rods

You can also use blaze rods as a source of fuel. One blaze rod will fuel the furnace for 120 seconds and can allow you to smelt or cook 12 items.

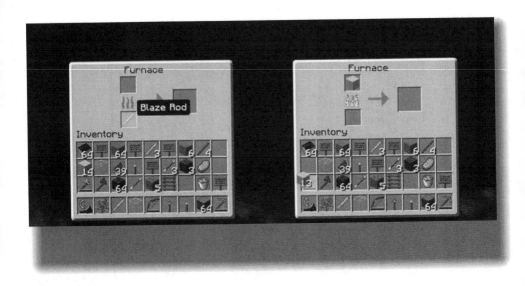

Burn All the Items

If you're in a bind though and need immediate fuel, remember that you can use any item from your inventory in your furnace as long as it is made of wood.

So if there's nothing to burn, use trapdoors, doors, ladders, saplings and even sticks to smelt.

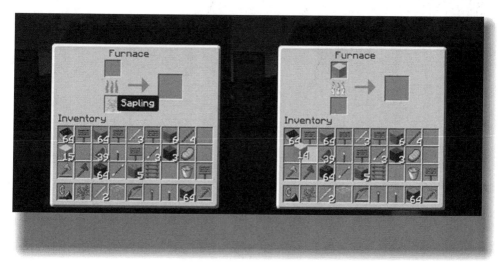

Use All Your Tools

In Minecraft, you can use different tools for different things but when you're harvesting, you don't just need to use the hoe.

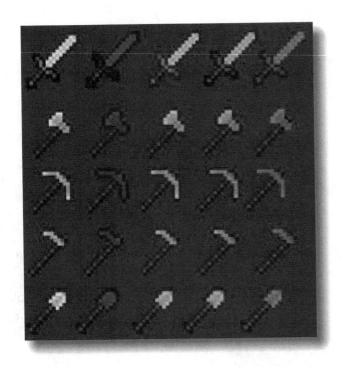

Alternate Axes

While axes help you chop wood faster, you can also

get pumpkins faster if you use an axe to do so.

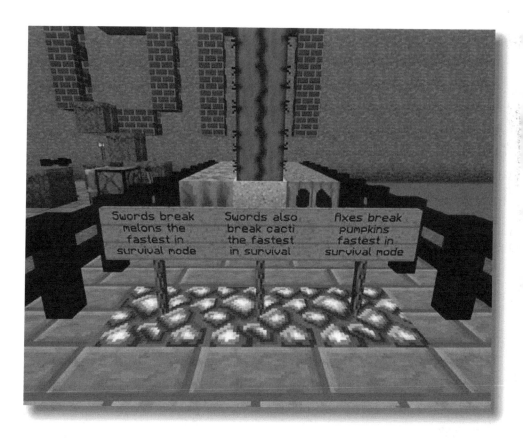

Killing Some Veggies

On the other hand, if you want to harvest some watermelon or a cactus, using a sword will give you faster results.

Using Slab Stones

Minecraft slabs have a lot of creative uses to them.

You can even try out these neat tricks with half

slabs of stones

Slab of Safety

If there are half slabs lying around, you might incidentally help out a few zombies.

If they're standing on a slab, Zombies will not burn, even if the sun is shining brightly.

Be warned though, they're still going to attack you

regardless of whether you just saved their lives or

not.

The Taming Game

Animals in Minecraft can be tamed but you have to

know how to do it.

Farm Animals

For livestock like sheep, pigs, cows and chicken, you need some wheat.

However, you better build a pasture otherwise they will just wander or roam away once the wheat is gone.

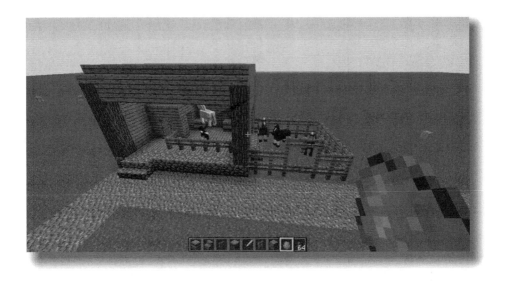

Giddy Up, Cowboy!

For horses, you need a saddle. However, if you come across one and you don't have a saddle ready, just tame it by hopping on it.

Keep doing it until the horse finally shows the heart icon. You just tamed your horse. You will still need the saddle though if you want to ride it around.

Man's Best Friend

You can tame wolves by offering them bones. You can get the bones by killing zombies or skeletons. You will need around 6 to 10 bones since you will have to offer them to the wolf a few times.

Once it shows the heart icon and a collar appears around its neck, you can walk your tamed wolf-dog home with you.

You can also tame as many wolves as you want so

get yourself a dog or two.

They will also attack any mobs or monsters who harm you or whom you attack so they're good to have by your side.

Here Kitty Kitty Kitty!

Ocelots can also be tamed if you offer them raw fish. They can also offer you protection from certain mobs as well.

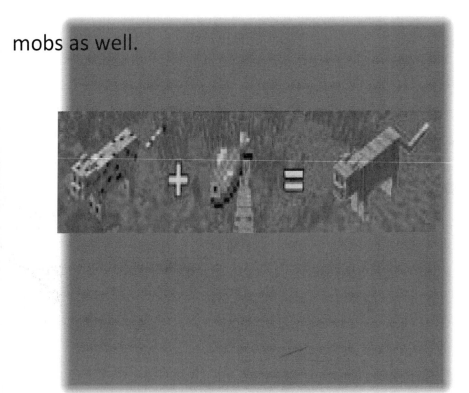

Creepers in particular are terrified of ocelots and will not approach them even when they aren't tamed.

Ocelots, once tamed will change color and look like domestic cats.

Summoning Games

In Minecraft you can also build some creepy

creatures with the weirdest materials.

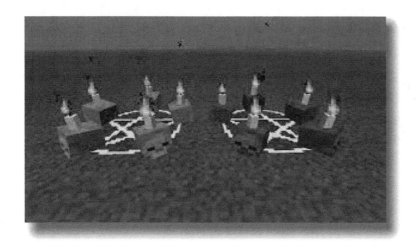

Do You Want to Build a Snowman?

If you want to build a snowman, you can make one using blocks of snow.

Pile two blocks of snow on top of each other and then use a Pumpkin for a head.

The Iron Man

If a snowman wasn't weird enough of for you, you can also make an iron golem which comes to life.

Take 4 blocks of iron and place them together. Now add the pumpkin as a head and watch your monstrosity come to life.

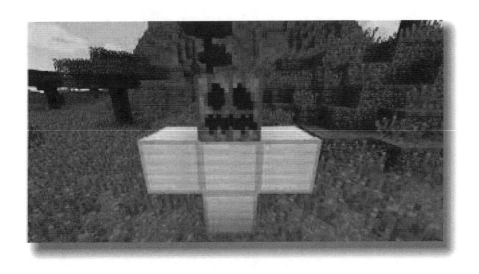

Release the Wither!

If the snowman and iron golem were too boring, then how about summoning the Wither?

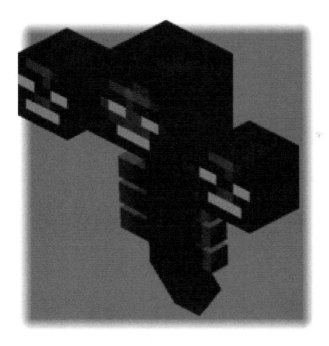

You will need to take a trip to the Nether to get the materials. All you need are three Wither skulls, harvested from Wither Skeletons and 4 blocks of Soul Sand.

Make a T shape with the soul sands and place the Wither skulls on top. Now get ready for a tough battle to take place.

Boost Your Crops

If you're tired of waiting for your crops to grow and want to speed them up, you can use some bonemeal to do so.

Bonemeal can be crafted with the help of bones or collected by killing Zombies and Skeletons. It's hard to get bonemeal so use it with precaution and in emergencies only.

Watery Lawn Mower

Tired of using the hoe to get rid of all that pesky grass? Just pour water over it all and call it a day.

No seriously, all the grass will be gone and you'll have a clear patch of land to build or play golf on.

Always Float to the Top

Water might slow down some mobs but it won't kill them. Mobs have the ability to float in water. They will also swim across or float across rivers and lakes.

If they walk into water, they will always float to the top. If you're building a moat, consider placing a row of blocks around it or making it really deep to make it harder for the mobs to get out.

A Beacon of Light

If you are feeling particularly lazy or don't have enough resources, you can use your beacon as a source of light.

Even if it is not activated, a beacon gives off greater light than torches. Don't hide it inside your home, put it to good use!

Enchanting Weapons

Minecraft allows you to enchant items as well so don't skip over this option. Enchanted weapons and tools can yield some really impressive things.

Not only do they improve your damage and defense, they also make it easier to collect resources.

Battle Axe

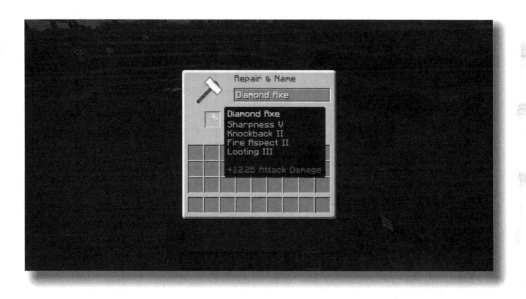

With the help of an Anvil and some enchanted books, you can but a weapons enchantment on your axe. This not only makes it useful for cutting down trees, you can now also use it to chop off a few zombie heads as well.

Magic Shears

If you think shears are just good for collecting wool, then think again.

With the help of an Anvil and few special enchantments like the Silk Touch, you can make your shears good to harvest anything.

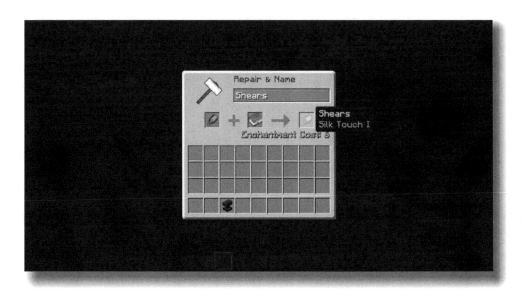

From grass to leaves, ferns and flowers, your enchanted shears will now allow you harvest anything you want.

Mash Them Up

If you have too many enchanted books which are just taking up important space in your inventory, don't dump them.

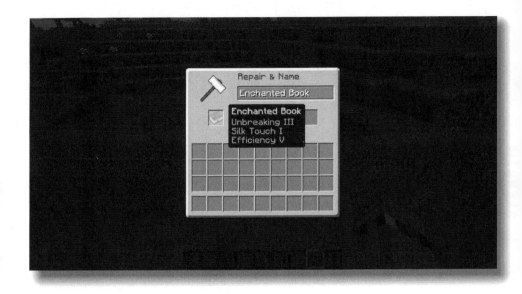

Use the Anvil and mash them all together to create

one, super awesome enchanted book. This frees up

space and gives you all you need in one book form.

Powerful Enchantments

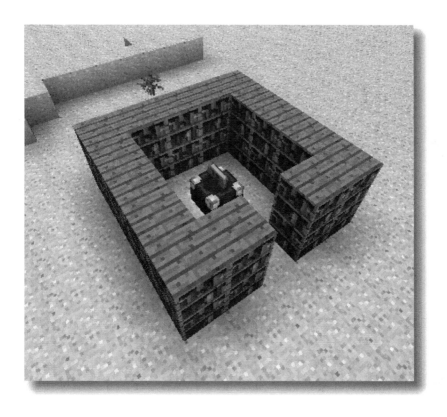

If you want to upgrade your enchantments, make sure that your enchanting table is surrounded by plenty of bookshelves.

Made in the USA
Middletown, DE
19 December 2015